I0753532

FINISHING LINE PRESS
www.finishinglinepress.com

A THOUSAND RAINBOWS FLASHING

poems by

Pattie Palmer-Baker

Finishing Line Press
Georgetown, Kentucky

A THOUSAND RAINBOWS FLASHING

ISBN 979-8-89990-507-0 First Edition

ACKNOWLEDGMENTS

Widening Circles, Pulp Literature Press Humming Bird first prize 2025

Publisher: Leah Huete de Maines
Editor: Christen Kincaid
Cover and Interior Art: Pattie Palmer Baker; Photographed by Patrick Smith
Author Photo: Robert R. Sanders
Cover Design: Elizabeth Maines McCleavy

Order online: www.finishinglinepress.com
also available on amazon.com

Author inquiries and mail orders:
Finishing Line Press
PO Box 1626
Georgetown, Kentucky 40324
USA

Contents

We write because there's real comfort in acknowledging that everything is always falling apart. We write to put what is broken back together, or better yet, to fashion the pieces into new, evermore beautiful shapes. We write to make tiny gifts that friends and strangers can hold in their hands.

Elizabeth H. Cottrell

SO MANY KINDS OF DARK

Penumbra

A shadow, smoky grey shot
through with scintilla
incense-saturated mist
wraps my body in
in a feather embrace

Umbra

The darkest part of a sunspot
count the many kinds of dark
black holes starless sky
my husband's lost words
his failed movements

When you listen, when you understand, you slide into me, erase my serrated edges, smooth my roughened heart

QUESTION FOR THE HEART

So, I ask my heart that once
pulsed red sparks and my blood

glowed sequined crimson when my
now dead husband said I love you,

has your magnificent magenta
faded to reddish-brown,

do you pump sluggish
muffled maroon blood

to circle around an indifferent
crumbling body, muscles

slack, sinews sagging, skin
shriveled too long waiting

for his now off-duty
presence, his absent touch.

To avoid going crazy from a sightfull of daisies, I order my gaze to form a straight
line, but her eyes have a mind their own and skitter to daffodils blinking
off she will escape from a spring flower gape

RED AND PURPLE ROSES

Sun ignites the dented river,
cupped flames of white-gold.

If I dive in, I will swim
in liquid crystal, but those

blazing hollows will burn
me to a shimmering image.

Better to walk on, pet a golden Pitbull.
He strains and ripples his muscles

to reach my paltry body. To kiss me.
He slams into my arms, my wrists

where red and purple roses now
bloom in a blue-veined garden.

the light nets in pollen, spores, wind strips the trees, sequined leaves, dust motes, glitter, pyrite gold, wind drinks the cream from the blue-gray sky
the sun is powering down

QUARKS AND LEPTONS

Do you think, I ask the pigeon
flashing iridescent green and pink

and the sky bleeding white
streaks across the pastel blue

and the wind-dented river
where my husband disperses

in the miniature hollows
sun-struck brilliant,

that quarks and leptons
really exist in this massive

universe and, if so, what do
they mean? What do they do?

Are they part of us, our
organs, like our heart?

Are they so nanoscopic they
have no eyes no body

no heart to beat rhythmically
the message, you are alive,

you are alive. Even when
you think you are dead.

NO BONES

My husband died June 19.
So dear to me so dear to me.

He did not pass away,
He did not float up

into the gray-blue stratosphere
or wing his way to angel-

occupied pious clouds.
He died. His body is not

underground waiting for the
bones to shine through.

Instead, flash fire consumed
him. Now ashes and bits

of bones pack into
a cardboard container.

PEWTER

Do you believe, I ask the wind-ruffled
Willamette River that beauty is in

the eye of the beholder? And not
everyone feels her throat tighten

when the wind, brisk with anxiety, crumples
the center of your water into a gold-glitter

disturbance so shimmering
I have to squint my eyes to see

or when the wind slows to almost stillness
and slicks you with satiny swathes of pewter

the color of my mother's eyes although not
as deeply hued except in my memory?

I believe in trees, not God, not angels, although leafed, tree branches would be their wings. the good don't go to heaven, their souls glide into oaks, aspens, maples, elms and birches where they wind round and round until they reach the heart of the tree

THE TREES ARE NOT DYING

Does it hurt, I ask the maple,
sumac, dogwood, gingko

when red slow-burns your leaves
when yellow usurps green

when gold devours chlorophyll
when orange fights with carmine

when coral eats chunks
of scarlet when the sun

shoots radiant shock-
waves into your core

when the sun forces
unwanted transparency

when crimson incandescence
incinerates all other colors

when dreary dead leaves
sag in a dirty yellow skirt

around your grieving trunk?

I CANNOT KISS THE SKY

Luminous indigo floods the sky,
a sky that holds my mother,

her memory. No that's not it.
She is the sky, that shimmering

purple-blue. I cannot
gather it in my arms,

I cannot kiss it, I
cannot even touch it.

Come back, Momma,
please comeback. Curl your

hand with the accident-
damaged fingers into mine,

press your soft barely fuzzed
cheek next to mine.

Call me dear.

Less body than ravens, crows shine the same black magic. Sleek bodies, sharp beaks, clever feet—so deep the mystery of their black feathers! Long ago they gathered in a murder so large they blocked out the sun. And night was born

BLACK SATIN

I wonder, I say to
the double-breasted

Cormorant, who unfurls
his black velvet wings

to dry in the morning
slice of blinding sun

floating on the blue steel
of the Willamette River

why some revile you as a
voracious nuisance who devours

more than your fair share of salmon
steelhead and tiny bottom fish

and never see that sleek
black-satin yellow-beaked

body dive into the water's
welcoming embrace deep

so deep you punch
through the bitter

brawling barrier
between light and dark

nor seldom notice
the blue of your eyes

almost but not quite the star-
sapphire blue my husband's.

A THOUSAND RAINBOWS

Do you think I ask the crow who snares
me in his right black-sheened eye

and the sun-struck river who flows
forever his rippled self to the sea,

our shadows are fragments
of dark matter that follow

our birth into a world indifferent
to mother-love tear-shined light?

Does dark matter even exist?
Scientists say this substance

without form swirls around our
world never touching the earth's

reality, yet sometimes I feel
a fingerless caress on my forearm

and glimpse my shadow behind me,
a slice of dark matter whispering

let go, let go. Merge with your
dead husband's shadow

which is not dark but
a thousand rainbows flashing.

LIPSTICK RED

my fingers obey my inner heart
(not the one fibrillating atrially
but the heart far from bodily control
or any kind of control at all
fingers tap tap tap mother momma father daddy
just when I want to write about roses
how their fragrance saturates the air
and the blooms fold out in full bodied layers
(not blue-touched just red clear and pure)
the color of the lipstick my mother wore
always she was never without
her nails too

The sprayer power-mists poison clouds over the Linden trees. Fifty thousand bumblebees, downdrift and soft-plop on the asphalt. Nearby the
colonies hunker in ground holes, queens and drones whisper confusion and wait. No workers, not one floats down
the hollowed passageways. The queens dream of fuzzed carapaces tumbling into a funeral pyre, and follow the curl of amber-streaked smoke, fly into
the fire's center, shoot out gold-barbed fireworks, stinging the onlookers blind.

ONE OF TWENTY THOUSAND

Do you think I ask the honey bee
swirling through the yellow dillweed

and the bumblebee bristling gold and
black in the towering sunflowers,

I would be better off, all humans
would be better off if we were

not one of one but one of many,
one of maybe twenty thousand

with our jobs, our sex lives (if any)
inked into our DNA, our whole

purpose would throb in our arms, our legs
our brains, our heart to love the whole,

we would not care if one or two
or even fifty dies, we would just

go on doing our job like picking
ripe almost red oranges to place

with a gentle, a feathery touch
in the palms of outstretched

hands trembling with ravenous
anticipation, eyes avid to eat

the color before their mouths devour
the deep brilliant sweetness and no one

says thank you thank you or even
sees the other as a one of them

and even if they could individuate
why would they hum a gratitude hymn?

Now the snake lies slack, its length checked by one loose coil. Still something to look at, though dead, two yellow stripes race up the slippery black; eyes shine ruby red. My heart continues to see such terrible beauty stilled: Sinewy strength once:

POETIC SNAKE

The snake writes poetry in S curves swirled on the earth's floor. He sings a soundless song rhyming every third word. All things living on the ground dance to the silent beat. He is beautiful to those who will look, to those who don't hate grounded things. Enameled in unsung colors, smooth to the touch, some hide in tool sheds, some sun on gray stones, their colors shine in the early morning milky light. Spiral decorated sculptures, a terrible beauty that can wound. His bite can kill. Sometimes. The devil chose this form to seduce Eve, she fell in love with the pure muscular form pulsing against her palm, she listened to his silky words, held out her sun-kissed hand where he placed the crimson-shined apple.

Not a pond toy, the beautiful koi. They have that rare ability, who just by being (oh those golden rays, those pearls gleaming) reveal the meaning of the phrase 'carpe diem'. I saw one black as carbon, all four momentarily united nuzzle the hand feeding him. Have you ever heard of one so brave (or was it love?) to risk air-drowning for a moment's touch.

SIXTY PERCENT OF ME

So, I say to the river,
thank you thank you

for your unruffled surface,
for your silky serenity.

Two days ago you ranted,
sharp-edged wavelets rose up

then fell into angry yellow-
white foam-topped valleys.

If I dove into that rage-driven
soot-gray water, the calculating

current would have devoured me
without knowing I too am water,

sixty percent of me.

Erratic oval elongated eye level lunatic moon man in the moon laughs and laughs offers me a drink I am drunk both of us are sliding off the sky my body shines moonbeams that slither through the night I swallow the moon my body opens my heart floats out a new moon

SOMETIMES GOLD

Don't worry I say to the
moon fat with silver

no one cares about the
gray patches pitting

your pearlescent surface.
We gaze eyes agape,

hearts tipping when
you shine your full

sometimes gold self,
in that purple-black sky,

some of us even open
our starving mouths

to swallow you, a communion
wafer floating out of reach.

Cold-shredded cloud down drift in silken motion. Almost weightless each sparkle-feather touch. I would rest my head on a white mound, let my body sink into a snow shroud. My last breath in fractured stars...

WIDENING CIRCLES

So, I ask the Canada goose
perched in front of his mate,

his coffee-colored wings
fanned out to hide his only

love from the seagull's stilled
menace, what will you do

when she is gone, dead or lost
in a cloud's chiffon swelling?

Will you fly in widening circles
until you orbit the whole world?

Will you forever feel her absence
in the hollow of your bones?

My husband's body is gone
my husband's body is ashes

but my skin still feels the
feathered trace of his fingers.

SHINING PATH

I apologize, I say to snail
for deeming you lethargic.

You live in a universe
of motion-slowed time,

coat of arms spiraled in fragile
armor. You trail jeweled ribbons

over a jagged road. When
a breeze threatens to unglue

your glide, you hunch and
buckle over the jutting brick,

you glitter, *what's the point?*
in your slime-slickened track.

Above, the near naked maples
parse your question, answer

in breeze-softened tones,
your pathway gleams.

THE REINCARNATION OF RAIN

I wonder, I ask the rain
sliding through the yielding

gray in silken streams
then spreading a darkening

sheet on the waiting asphalt
melding into adjoining ponds,

if when the wind gathers
up your last glitters,

do you realize you are not
dead, you are not gone?

You are transubstantiated
into a thing with no volume

no shape, you are free
to roam the vastness

until you coalesce again into water
suspended in the sky's netting

waiting to distill into drops
floating falling plummeting

to the welcoming ground
to the hallowed earth.

PEARLS THROUGH SILK

Do you think, I ask the Canadian
goose feathered in muted earth tones,

if I hollow my bones
and fold out my arms

into brown-gray plumaged
wings, I will lift up up up

and fly into ruffled clouds,
white-blinded and lost?

In a breathy baritone tone
I will call out where am I, where?

I will hear hundreds of wings
like micro breezes whoosh nearby,

and a trumpeted response,
follow us follow us.

Will you fly me to my husband
who can't, no can't be dead?

He flies also, I know this, but too
high to reach, too high to see.

I want to soar up, find him
and enfold him in my wings,

press him against my
softly rounded breast.

We will plummet through the earth
like pearls through silk to the other

side of now, where stars blaze,
rainbows shimmer and darkness is dead.

For many years, *Pattie Palmer-Baker* exhibited mixed-media artwork that fused paste-paper collage with her poetry rendered in calligraphic form. Paste paper—an ancient decorative art created by manipulating pigments mixed with specially prepared paste on wet paper—became both her medium and metaphor. From these richly textured surfaces, she cut intricate shapes and images that intertwined with her poems written around the edges of the work, creating pieces that invited viewers to read as much as to look.

Over time, however, something unexpected happened: audiences often found themselves lingering over the poems as long as, or longer than, the artwork itself. What began as a visual practice gradually revealed itself to be a literary one. Encouraged by those responses, Palmer-Baker devoted herself to writing poetry, bringing with her the same precision, layering, musicality, and visual imagination that shaped her art.

Her poetry has since appeared in numerous journals and anthologies, including *Bacopa Literary Review, Military Experience and the Arts, Ghazal Page, Voices: The Art and Science of Psychotherapy, Calyx,* and *Phantom Drift.* Twice nominated for the Pushcart Prize, her work has been recognized for its emotional depth, lyrical intensity, and originality. Her honors include First Prize in the *Timberline Review* contest (2016), the Bivona Prize in the *Ageless Authors Anthology* (2019), First Prize in the Oprelle Oxbow Contest (2022), and First Prize from Pulp Literature Press (2025).

She is the author of the chapbook *The Color of Goodbye* (Kelsay Press, 2021), and the full-length poetry collection *Five Fundamental Forces* (MoonPath Press, 2023). Across both page and image, her work explores memory, loss, resilience, and the hidden currents that connect inner and outer worlds, always with an artist's eye for texture, rhythm, and luminous detail.

www.ingramcontent.com/pod-product-compliance
Lightning Source LLC
LaVergne TN
LVHW052310100826
845147LV00006B/721

9798899905070